Love and other Mysteries

Love and other Mysteries

MEGAN WILLOME

RESOURCE *Publications* · Eugene, Oregon

LOVE AND OTHER MYSTERIES

Resource Publications
An Imprint of Wipf and Stock Publishers
199 W. 8th Ave., Suite 3
Eugene, OR 97401

www.wipfandstock.com

PAPERBACK ISBN: 979-8-3852-3150-8
HARDCOVER ISBN: 979-8-3852-3151-5
EBOOK ISBN: 979-8-3852-3152-2
VERSION NUMBER 11/11/24

for John
for going round and round together with me for all these years

"The Spouse in the Canticles, unable to find her Beloved in the time of repose, went forth to seek Him in the city. But in vain ... it was only without the walls she found Him."

"LETTER XV TO CÉLINE: 2 AUGUST 1893,"
THE STORY OF A SOUL: THE AUTOBIOGRAPHY
OF ST. THÉRÈSE OF LISIEUX

Contents

SORROWFUL MYSTERIES

GLORIOUS MYSTERIES

Acknowledgements

Many thanks to Anna, Carol, Dave, Jody, and Sarah, who made this collection better by coming alongside me. And thank you, Callie, for inspiring me to write more than a few of these poems in one of your workshops.

With great gratitude to the editors who featured these poems in the following publications:

Bread: Autumn 2024 from Kosmeo Magazine: "Psalm 30: Flagless Memorial Day"

Renaissance Journal from The Way Back to Ourselves, Spring 2024: "Golden-cheeked Warbler" and "If I Step into the Light"

Summer Breeze from The ClayJar Review, June 21, 2024: "Pomegranate" and "Three Kisses at Pentecost"

The Windhover, 28.2, "Ephaphtha"

"Make Me Redbud" originally appeared at Chronic Joy (chronic-joy.org)

"The Pleiades and Orion" originally appeared at Ekstasis (ekstasis-magazine.com)

ACKNOWLEDGEMENTS

"Mrs. Blevins Prays As John Grady Cole Rides Away" originally appeared at Tweetspeak Poetry (tweeetspeakpoetry.com)

"Snow White," "Texas Squall," and "Top of the Rock," originally appeared in an earlier version at meganwillome.com

"Lost Prayers," "Magnificat," and "Psalm 145" originally appeared in an earlier version at Poetry For Life, meganwillome.substack.com

Beads, Songs, Poems, and Birds

An August weary. Muggy enough to call it hot by 7:45 in the morning. School has begun, and a group of parents gather around a fountain to pray the rosary. We meet for the first twenty-two days of school to pray for the twenty-two people who died in the shooting in nearby Uvalde, Texas.

I have been Catholic for ten years. I own the circle of beads that is a rosary, but I do not know how to pray with it. With these moms and dads, I meditate on the life of Jesus and his Blessed Mother, story by story, round and round the four Mysteries: **Joyful, Luminous, Sorrowful, Glorious.**

As I turn beads, I ponder my own mysterious turns. Like most folks in midlife, there has been loss as well as love. My parents, already gone. My children, grown and flown. My marriage, somehow good after three inexplicable decades. My relationship with Jesus, more duty than desire. There is within me a longing I cannot name.

"Whither has your beloved gone," says Song of Solomon 6:1. There's more to the verse, but I like ending it there, with a comma. The unendedness leaves room.

I've loved Song of Solomon since I was far too young for it. It always causes faith to rise in me. I am not a scholar, but a poet. When something moves me—a bird, a wildflower, a storm—I can't help but write a poem in response. I began wanting to poem my way through Song of Solomon after those days around the fountain, after I began praying the rosary myself, using a booklet published by the Knights of Columbus called *A Scriptural Rosary for the Family*. It's full of verses from Songs. I began writing love poems while reading Song of Solomon during a snowy retreat in Jackson Hole, Wyoming, visiting family.

Love is my grand conclusion from spilling pencil lead over the Canticle of Canticles. Shouldn't my takeaway from this ancient, erotic text be more theologically pure, less Juliet-esque? It is not.

I am far too old to seek this Lover now, like a bird I can't quite reach. Song of Solomon would use the image of a dove; I prefer a cardinal. A flash of red, whistling. Unwilling to leave me alone. Daring me to write my loves and mysteries into poems. Perhaps there is nothing more theological than eros.

My eight Songs poems, one for each chapter from Song of Solomon, form the backbone of this collection. The others are arranged according to the traditional Mysteries of the rosary. The Mystery and one of its fruits is listed at the beginning of each section. Those fruits are hiding in the text, waiting for you to seek them.

Several of the poems are about hikes (the ultimate searching activity). Some are written in my purest Texan voice. Most germinated in the rocky soil of my home—terrible for traditional crops, but good for something. Especially for wine.

Each of my life's mysteries stems from a story, and each story is its own mystery. Maybe our stories must include loss—of parents, partners, health, dreams—before we are open to a love never before dared. Love that loves us first, and we blush.

My prayers remain with the families of Uvalde. I cannot identify with their losses, but my dad had an empathy beyond my experience. He helped save lives during the school shooting at the University of Texas at Austin on August 1, 1966. That event never lost its mystery for him. I am grateful that, most days, he was able to love.

–MEGAN WILLOME

JOYFUL MYSTERIES

The Annunciation: humility

The Visitation: love of neighbor

The Nativity: detachment

The Presentation: purity

The Finding of Jesus in the Temple: joy

ALL

Psalm 145

For all the church, all the books, all the lazy Sunday afternoons,
 all the Psalms, all
the friends and all the calls and all the messages and all the coffee
 dates and all our dark
morning walks, for these sins as opposed to others, for all the
 graces I can scarcely tell
and even then, not all.

For all the poems pouring out after all that rain, for all the Yes's to
 my work and even
the No's when it wasn't all right, how all the things I don't know
 how to write about
become all the poems, for summer's tiny wildflowers, for every
 red wing, for cactus all
over these hills, even in drought, and all their prickly pear gold.

For every Mass, all the hours of Adoration when all I could do
 was weep, for all
the prayers answered and all the ones where you slept all night
 but slept right here,
in my boat, and bid me rest, and all the ways a storm rouses our
 blood and bids
our bodies get up and come outside and inhale all the charged
 molecules.

For hip bones, how my thorn pains me all the time whichever
 way I bend, and for lace
and every $3 sundress from St. Vinny's, for a rocking chair
 bought when I was first

pregnant that still cradles all of me, for all the snowflakes at my
    birthday picnic,
and, obviously, all the dogs.

For all my saints (you know who you are). For all angels who sing
    along. For bread, wine,
and all I do not understand. For every word of pink story, ever
    raveling into a beautiful shield,
fit for all that meets me today.

DUET

Songs 1

And Jesus says, *I have something for you.*
And Mary says, *Is it an allegory?*
And Jesus says, *I prefer stories.*
And Mary says, *Is it a parable?*
And Jesus says, *It's passed under a desk, played over candlelight, danced at a wedding.*
And Mary says, *Remember our wedding?*
And Jesus says, *Um, you know how I love marriage, but ...*
And Mary says, *You know what I mean! The one with your wine.*
And Jesus says, *Oh yes! Woman, this is a love song.*
And Mary says, *Won't they misunderstand? I only want them to see you.*
And Jesus says, *I'll bury it in the Old Testament. Hey, I'll give it to Solomon. Ha!*
She says, *But some will get it, right?*
Yes, He says, *Some.*

MARIENKIRCHE

Fredericksburg, Texas

she wears a black lace mantilla
soft toes make tile sing
blue window-clouds glow from white walls
pews groan—wooden humility—
handles crackle as door unsticks
lets in windsong   flowerbreath
shuffling beads   shuffling bodies
children noisy as church bells
tourists lift cameras to altars
snap snap snap
sunlight offers homily
she smiles at St. Joseph,   his illustrious lily
angels breathe loud enough to notice
wrens clap amen from nests hidden high
let them say she never recovered   but still   she sang

The Annunciation

WINTERPAST

Songs 2

I'd recognize your truck anywhere
    (I know where you usually park)
    I fake reasons to drive past your house

Once I saw you on a Thursday morning
    came back: same time, same spot,
    desperate to catch your eye again (your wildflower smile)

(God in Heaven) once I glimpsed you
    in fresh-pressed jeans and boots and I was ready
    to leave everything everyone follow you everywhere

Your words are saved in a secret place
    telling me things I already know
    (I pretend not to know)

One winterpast I saw your name on a playlist
    and now I can't not see your name every time
    I pull it up (I often pull it up)

Like that tune about mistletoe, the one stuck on repeat,
    every note how I feel when I'm with you
    (wordless)

MAGNIFICAT

A woman in skinny jeans, ballet flats,
blue coat, black veil,
sits on the front row—a rare Mass
without her family.
For one hour she sits in herself.
Not a doctor, not a wife or a mother,

not anything but a woman
who came on a Friday at noon,
hungry as Eve. Her eyelashes ponder
the Mary statue in the corner.
She cannot imagine a future without
piano, no apple slices, no lost shoes,

only this neighbor who somehow
overwhelms her tall frame
with a frantic grey hug and charity
the older one does not deserve
(and she knows it) but
they both know this inner leaping,
these boys who will not stay still.

The Visitation

KATY, BAR THE DOOR

Job 38:8–10

No mystical rose, she—a mother
four times over. No one told her
when she entered the bramble-thicket
of birth her body would become
a chord coiled, a gate to unleash
ocean, and then
—detachment—
her at one end of the pew,
him at the other, divided by
children. Sorrow smiles on her
constant and prudent
as the morning star. She kneels tall,
a tower of ivory. After Communion,
five golden minutes of silence—
here in this vessel, an unspooling.
She kneels next to him.
He kneels next to her.
Their mirrored backs venerable
in the fractals of color heaving
through morning's stained glass.
O God, for this mother,
Send in the clouds.

The Nativity

LOST PRAYERS

"I leave my prayers in odd places, too."
–Jody L. Collins, "What Had Been Lost," *Mining the Bright Birds*

Like beside the baby grand,
the one I stand next to and sing,
kneel next to and cry a cussing prayer
and, I guess, got good
and heard because now I can't find my prayers.

They're not in the piano bench.
Not by the lamp
or under the pew. Maybe they blew
out the Mary door into the garden—
swords piercing purity's soil.

Maybe they will become tree.

O lost prayers,
I do not know what kind of forest you will be.

The Presentation

THE PLEIADES AND ORION

"No, Orion! No, Pleiades!" barks a small woman
    at two hulking black dogs who lunge at me.

We all walk early, before dark turns to morning,
    before most dog owners set out.

I walk on the opposite side of the road.
    The hunter and his prey sense dog-scent on me

though I walk without dogs.
    They know the cords that bind me to Orion,

the chains that link me to seven starry daughters.
    Again, day darkens into night. Some wake with divine

mercy, some slumber under constellations.
    All of us made.

All of us chasing, chasing, chasing.

TOP OF THE ROCK

Rockefeller Center, New York City

Seventy floors above, worries
for you
I exit through the gift shop
tsking at tchotchkes
when—oh joy!—I spy
a deck of playing cards
and I want them for you
who brought cards on every trip
made me play Go Fish when we missed our plane.
We've missed every plane,
boat, taxi, gondola,
elevator ascending above the Rainbow Room,
spaceship.
See my binoculars above the city?
I looked for you everywhere.

The Finding of Jesus in the Temple

LUMINOUS MYSTERIES

The Baptism of Christ: openness to the Holy Spirit
The Wedding Feast at Cana: to Jesus through Mary
Jesus' Proclamation of the Kingdom of God: conversion
The Transfiguration: desire for holiness
The Institution of the Eucharist: adoration

SNOW WHITE

I knew what I was doing,
walking a tightrope
strung between men and apples.

I only wanted
true love's taste on my tongue.

ENCHANTED ROCK STATE NATURAL AREA

Fredericksburg, Texas

The legend said
the park held
spirits but we
came anyway. Because
wildflowers. Got lost
on the Loop
Trail, failed to
make a perfect
circle. Found every
cave. Scaled granite's
dome, crested breathless.
Studied crevices, ponds,
each an ecosystem.
You skipped downhill.
I descended slow
as fast as
ever I could.

MOUNTAIN HOUSE

Estes Park, Colorado

Listen
In the twilight
To your very own
Tune dip,
Lilt, across the porch, all
Eyes on you, your guitar below the

Bear statue where each note
En-blues the night and your fingers become
Anthem and you
Rise into your private constellation

BUENA VISTA / BIBLE POINT

Rocky Mountain National Park

I can't take it anymore, I said and piled us
into my new red car with the moonroof. Left Texas.
Drove through Oklahoma until, finally, Colorado.

I remember the drive more than the days,
the skateboard at rest areas, the stories on CD,
this darkling thrush, singing away the miles.

I don't know when Buena Vista became Bible Point,
when the Buddhist monks stopped their dawn prayers,
what the high school marching band played as sun rose

on our last day of vacation. Nests or mountains? That
is the question. We snapped a selfie at the mini-golf,
leaned against a trap shaped like a house.

TEXAS SQUALL

Lord knows a storm's gotta break sometime.
It knows it's needed
when sorrows
can't cloud up one moment more
and you set there on the porch
prayin you at least get some rain
outta this storm
dang it
cuz so far it's just lightnin
lightin up the sky
looks like the trees are lyin to you
till all hail breaks loose
like someone's hurlin
baseballs golf balls grapefruit oranges
every size of round right at you.

Next mornin
live oak limbs litter streets
car windows all busted out
skylights broken
you got threshed but good and all
anyone can talk about is how that pollen's gone.
Clean gone.

C'mon out, y'all

THE WINDOW

Big Bend National Park

I hike this trail alone—
down, down, down. When it rains

all the water in the Chisos Basin pours
off this ledge, rocks slippery when dry.

The Rio Grande never fills. A fall
would be fatal. Some hiker guy gives

me his spot on the ledge. I sit solitary,
held fast by polished stone. A Mexican jay

sings what I can't decipher as I remember
another bright Valentine's Day when we

hiked Pedernales Falls after the floods.
Before I could yell *Don't* you'd already

leapt between boulders. You saw him first,
the man with the new leg, who helped

his pit bull navigate each slick space.
For 127 minutes I straddle choices until

a deluge unlocks me and I take the plunge
out of this desert openness
after the wild goose.

The Baptism of Christ

WHATEVER

Songs 3

To all the people in Battlin' Billie country
the priest announces in an accent never before heard:
GOD IS LOVE.
Everything He made is good. Especially love.
And marriage especially. All us

Jesus people—married and not so much, deaf to love,
impoverished hearts—try to fix love's waves

Through sheer willpower. As if a plunge into blue
could wrangle a sea-change. As if one might forsake
love as the tide rolls out and never
feel it roll back again. To all these,

Mary says, *Whatever.* Mermaids from
the wine-dark sea chorus, *All you people,*
lovers of showers and roses, be careful
when you throw a penny in love's ocean.

The Wedding at Cana

GIT 'ER DONE

Daddy—I still call him that
—can you cut this bath bomb in half?

He carries away the lavender ball
from the kitchen, its knives,

out to my truck, opens the tailgate,
sets in place the delicate sphere,

all acid and bicarbonate.
First he tries a hacksaw.

Then a real saw. This job needs
trust and a chainsaw's

tractable mechanical teeth.
Once the whole severs

into sheared moons, one
in each shutting hand,

only then can conversion
fizz.

Jesus' Proclamation of the Kingdom of God

LOST MAPLES STATE NATURAL AREA

Vanderpool, Texas, 54 miles from Uvalde

Easter means a hike, a seven-mile loop
with kids in single digits at the state park
where all lost things are found, even maples
with no business thriving in the heart of Texas.

Atop the bluff: two brave backpacks
stuffed with holy desire
for paths unmarked.

The horizon
already misty.

The Transfiguration

PSALM 123

after "It Was a Beauteous Evening, Calm and Free"
by William Wordsworth

It was a summer morning, still and hot.
Men were working, tearing up old tile.
I came early, to practice for a while—
free and calm and almost beauteous—
sang, and all my troubles I forgot,
sang despite contempt, despite each scourge,
sang into what was an empty church:
eyes perched for God: his step, melodious.
And then the door blew open. In they came.
Their eyes on me, their ears on my lament,
my eyes on them, to sing some glorious favor.
Her eyes on him, her heart with love aflame.
He listened to my song. He did not waver.
And now my soul pours ever in ascent.

FOOL'S GOLD

Water
Sugar
Yeast
Your ugliest peaches

Boil
Combine
Ferment
Filter
Ferment
Pour into new wineskins
Ferment some more
Bottle
Let rest for a year
Watch in adoration

Uncork summer
Sip what hail hath made
Serve with sourdough
from everlasting levain

The Institution of the Eucharist

THREE KISSES AT PENTECOST

Songs 4

For wildness like this I need snapdragons—
no, not fiery enough. Dragonwing begonias
begotten from your hand. And tulips.
(flaming parrot, perhaps?) Geraniums
to hang from my porch. You, sir, know how
to bubble my fountain. You uncork my perfumes
that do not come from a bottle. You have found
every wild beast on my heights. Wash me
with your *I love yous*. Gimme gladiolas,
if you've got them. I want all your love,
from A to zinnia. Take my arms,
full of carnations for you, my friend.
Make us wine—instantly old. Shall we
meet where the *pfingstrose* blooms?
Where whispers the peony wind.

MRS. BLEVINS PRAYS AS JOHN GRADY COLE RIDES AWAY

There he goes, off on some horse, like my boy,
a fool for bowlin alleys, horses, guns, a mean
ol mule, hard of heart. Damn near destroyed
us. But Jimmy Blevins Gospel Hour's clean
heard to Timbuktu, France, South Pole, Mars.
Criminals in Mexican prisons'll barter for a radio
just to hear the falsetto cry of Jimmy Blevins. Man's
wore out. Never thought a fella'd come to Del Rio
on some big bay and not ask for no blessin.
Just eat my cobbler, ma'am me, not ask questions.
Nice boy. Not one for conversation.
People have no idea how long we been prayin.
I didnt say nothin bout which of us was missin
cuz Sweet Jesus, the poor darlin just might be listenin.

SORROWFUL MYSTERIES

The Agony in the Garden: obedience

The Scourging at the Pillar: mortification

The Crowning with Thorns: courage

The Carrying of the Cross: patience

The Crucifixion: forgiveness of enemies

PSALM OF THE MOTHER IN THE FIERY FURNACE

Daniel 3:52–90

Blessed are you, Father
> How long is this here long obedience, do you reckon?

Blessed are you, Jesus
> Our friend in flame

Blessed are you, Spirit
> Flying wild

Blessed are you, Church
> Unbreakable pecan space between sanctuaries

Blessed are you, angels
> Disguised in sleek kits, on carbon bikes, pulling me over the big hill

Blessed are you, sun
> For light's color

Blessed are you, moon
> So many, many poems

Blessed are you, waters
> Super-waters somewhere, just not here, not now

Blessed are you, Leviathan
> Who hooked me by the tongue

Blessed are you, wind
> Ungraspable though I swing my butterfly net

Blessed are you, trees
> Bumblebees in your branches

Blessed are you, wildflowers
> Who cling with tiny green riffles

Blessed are you, snow
> Oh how I miss your smile on the pumpkins

Blessed are you, thunder and lightning
> And every time I walked in the dark and was not struck

Blessed are you, granite boulders
    Ever-poised to fall, you pause
Blessed are you, lark sparrows
    Hymn-writers
Blessed are you, trauma-puppy
    Trembling at love
Blessed are you, oh my dead
    More real than salt
Blessed are you, words
    I am great with pencil
Bless the Lord, you women of sorrows,
    Every mother, bless your heart

The Agony in the Garden

NOT MILLS LAKE

Rocky Mountain National Park

We intended to hike to Mills Lake. Truly.
Blame the doe elk, Mother of Loch Vale,
beacon who blocked our path and nudged
us straight up Glacier Gorge.

> We were wrong while we climbed
> Wrong while we picnicked
> Wrong while we made our wrong way down

Perhaps Wordsworth sent the Steller's jay
who scolded us. With bold hops, his black crest
jeered a blue streak of mortifications that
we could not yet hear.

The Scourging at the Pillar

CIBOLO CREEK

Boerne, Texas

We feed the ducks
Our uneaten lunch
We do not speak
We sit beside the Sunday creek

Our lunches, uneaten
An hour is a million minutes
We walk along the Sunday creek
Don't mention such bad luck

Two hours is two million minutes
Courage dwells in cypress roots
Let's not mention our bad luck
Deer turn as our shoes squeak

But we, we shall not speak
Of courage hid in cypress roots
No more food for ducks
Turn, dear. Hear her shoe squeak?

The Crowning with Thorns

SOLSTICE

Songs 5

1

You were in my dream
beside me, a new bride
wide awake in bed
awaiting
the longest day of the year.
I opened my eyes—reached
—you were gone.

2

A little girl—lost. I take her to a house
with rooms. St. Joseph lies in bed
asleep. *Go to him*, I say, and she pulls
his arm over her, like a blanket. He
kisses her head. To me, he nods
with his eyes. They rest.

3

Soup's ready, I say.
He says, *I decline*, blocks
my words, my fountain of song.
I need coffee, a shower,
a beloved to lean on.

4

I am looking. I am lost. I am open
to almost any suggestion.
Like a cardinal, he whistles.
Like a nest, I wait, faint.

5
Where did he go? When I ask for help
Even friends shrug and whisper,
We want nothing to do with her.

6
Blessed midnight arrives. He grins,
Let's go. You're a pro.

7
O my Jesus, make me flight.

WRITER'S BLOCK IN THE KEY OF G MINOR

Show me? she says. He says,
Hear it: two sharps, no flats.

She needs to hear him touch
the piano. Adjacent chords click

tongue and groove. *G minor,*
he says. She says, *It shouldn't be there.*

It's possible, he says. She says
nothing because the key

to writing a song is knowing
which notes are available

and what is not.

SPEECHLESS

with Isaiah 35:1–10

Virgin speechless, her tongue a steppe.
She sits high and dry atop her tower.
Only in the dark does she venture out
to the highway. Come dawn,
walking along the road, a jackal crosses
her path, keeps his distance until dusk,
places paws on girl shoulders, kisses
—*You're so beautiful*—
turns up the volume on his eyes.

She does not flee.

He does, into the new moon.

Sleepless she sings wildflowers
all the long night and all the long nights
to come, ordinary obvious glory,
then kneels, howls.

BOO

"for the works of the LORD are wonderful,
and his works are concealed from men."

–SIRACH 11:4, RSVCE

The crib buried in the attic. The crawlspace
between pier and beam where we cannot
(will not) crawl. They say there's a glorious cache
in the oak—gum and pennies, pocket watch and medal,
children ensconced in soap. Today I imagine him
watching, working up a pair of cardinal children.
Where will he come by enough red paint? Jesus,
someone ought to give the man a hand up.
(Not me, surely, you see why not me.)
Summertime, fall, winter, winter, summer, autumn again.
All of us stuck. Here. Where First Purchase is as far from
the Methodists as you from me. It's a wonder, God, why,
with so many street lights at your command,
you work in the dark.

DEVIL'S BACKBONE

Wimberly, Texas

The school zones are the first to go.
Then traffic altogether.
Next, our need to hide. All patience,
we climb in the old white truck,
hit roads with no center stripe,

drive out Devil's Backbone, stunning
an hour past sunrise. Hills green as Ireland
complete with ditch-fog.
Pandemic?
Nature don't care. We curve
this one-hundred-twenty-four-mile loop.

God only knows how long
we have left.

The Carrying of the Cross

AFTER A DEATH, CLEANING
THE BATHROOM

Finally his bathroom I had to clean
scrub the cold tile floor
the last place he'd been.
I could do it. I'd done it before.
Breathe. Then spray.
Find a towel. Then wipe.
Do it well but look away. Forgiveness,
the one chore I've never liked.

Did the job. Used up the bleach.
Saw where he had hit the wall.
Erasure was within my reach—
not the man, but the fall.
With my sponge I kept caressing
until I had deterged a blessing.

The Crucifixion

MESQUITE

It's the best tree in the whole wide world! you said
of the trashy weed posing as a tree.
Last spring mesquite all over town threw a green bash,
fern leaves shaded during outdoor yoga. You wanted one

to guard your grave. And oh
how I love to see you smile.
But I don't need a tree to remember
how your roots spread for miles,

sucked every drop dry.
Your mesquite slit my redbud,
sir.
I cannot tell come here from sic'em.

CROW VILLANELLE

for Father Inna

The evening had an eerie glow.
We made your food, on this, your date.
We drove in search of you, your crow.

You'd come. You would. You'd say hello,
forget the past, forget your hate.
The evening had an eerie glow.

A feast for you we would bestow.
We looked all day. The time grew late.
We drove, still searching for your crow.

Come. Eat. What broke so long ago
'txist you and us—it wasn't fate.
Those evenings have an eerie glow.

And yet for you our heart still flows—
receive our gift. Please try. Partake.
We drove until we found your crow.

Our faces you still seemed to know.
You ate, then slipped right through the gate.
That evening—oh!—it's all aglow
when finally we found your crow.

PSALM 89, CHRISTMAS EVE VIGIL MASS

after "Wintering" by Sylvia Plath

This is the hard time, no doubt.
I have sung the yuletide carols,
I have my Ark,
Seven tokens of her,
Seven mother-swords for every sorrow-filled hour,

Waiting for Midnight Mass
Where I will sing with the choir
Above the Nativity creche
and artificial trees—
A still-empty manger.

The Vigil Mass is the one I have never been to
The Vigil Mass is the one I cannot bear.
All the noisy happy families,
Only chaos
On my phone, in my email

White space like tired snow—
Unused glitter. Emptiness.
Silence.
I am possessed.
It is no one's fault,

Not even mine.
This is the season of the rivers—the rivers
So bright I almost miss them,
Flashing like headlights
Into our four eyes

Each now dry from weeping.
Psalms of the Lord keep me going,
Each good note.
Even this psalm serves kindness, dark chocolate.
I suck it. Sweetness settles.

The river of congregants sing
Unison
Against their lonely shores.
Their flooded covenants.
Their "Christmas (Baby, Please Come Home)"

Love choruses, because it's Christmas
Eve and there is still time.
The Holy Child is unborn,
Blessed Mary is still in labor.
St. Joseph sticking by them,

Shepherds stumble under angel voices.
Christmas is for mothers—
One mother, a twin on either side,
Squirming themselves awake.
Her body a star farther than the sea and too stalwart to rest.

Will I make it to Midnight Mass, will I sing
Joy at The Nativity of the Lord though I do not know
How long?
How will I walk across this water?
Jesus is coming. He always comes.

"MARY WALKED THROUGH A WOOD OF THORN"

with the German carol

September. To escape the cricket apocalypse
we flee to the coast. The air smells toxic.
Paralyzed fish litter shores. The gulls are gone.
Our steps, cautious. Though red tides wax and wane
—the marine zoo recovers.

October. Before the art of aspens, worries fall
like catkins. Questions climb out the car window.
Too soon a too-early blizzard races us to the cabin,
where, leafless of winter gear, we huddle
—cocoa for two.

Christmas Day. With mourning doves I sing
carols with rosy young women. All of us rooted
from a single sapling. All of us heroines who leap
into fire's char and, sensing a crossroads, seed,
—beget gold.

"MAN STEALS HEART, NO CHARGES FILED"

(actual newspaper headline)
Songs 6

He strolls into my store, takes his time, ever browsing, never
    buying. *Did you make all this?*
        Yup.
You know what they say: Creativity is next to godliness
        I heard it Cleanliness.
That's a bad translation. This place of yours—so peaceful and sad
        I'm waiting for someone. All this is for them.
That's daunting. Have they come?
        Not yet. But I'm making something new. This is the one.
        They'll lay down their arms and come.
With arms you can dance as well as fight
        I guess.
It takes a lot of eros to create the way you do
        That's not exactly the kind of love I was going for.
        Please, sir, avert your eyes. They unsettle me.
You want what you can't have, so you want something else you can't
    have either
He palms a heart-shaped rock, winks, *I'll take this*, then strolls
    out the door, adding,
Hey, tonight there's a dance up on the mountain—a whole wedding.
Wanna come?
        I follow, leave my beloveds on the shelves, press no
        charges, only his hand

GLORIOUS MYSTERIES

The Resurrection: faith

The Ascension: hope

The Descent of the Holy Spirit: love of God

The Assumption: happy death

The Coronation of Mary: perseverance

MAKE ME REDBUD

after Abigail Carroll's "Make Me" poems

Make me redbud, not
too tall. Commonplace.
In winter, make barren
sparseness strength. Come
spring, bloom me purple
for a ladybug party. And
oh, through summer, so
searing and weary, keep
me green with eternal
song. Hold me high till
the breaking of autumn,
wind blowing gold breath.
So many heart-shaped
leaves! So many umbrella
branches! Let cardinals
find me, form family.
Make me shade.

BIERSTADT LAKE

Rocky Mountain National Park

My wedding ring, sir? Last seen at Bierstadt Lake,
where I took off my glove to eat a burrito (my bad)
and oops my ring came off with it. I have no faith
it'll be found after we stumbled over our snowshoes,
following orange flags until the parking lot appeared
finally.

   Ma'am, says the heron of a man presiding above
   the visitor center desk, a man too tall and too young
   to know anything of nuptials, *after the snow melts*
   you wouldn't believe how these things reveal themselves.

High summer. The Nativity of Saint John the Baptist.
The priest of the visitor center rings me up, *Ma'am,*
things always turn up when you stop expecting.

The Resurrection

WAITING FOR THE SPIRIT AFTER A SABBATH'S JOURNEY

with Acts 1 and "Stopping by Woods on a Snowy Evening" by Robert Frost

We made the long walk back to town.
The dirt was cracked and dry and brown.
The mountain—we could scarce conceive.
Our hesitating hearts, cast down.

Before he left, he said, *Don't leave.*
The Spirit you will soon receive.
And then he rose into the air.
Wait. Be filled, He said, *Believe.*

Angels came, but I felt bare.
Why look up? No hope, just prayer.
He's gone. How long? And no goodbye.
I stared at my shoe. I did not dare

to raise my eyes back up to sky.
We waited in the room up high.
His Mother's tales, they made us cry.
His Mother's tales, they made us cry.

The Ascension

IF I STEP INTO THE LIGHT

I might bloom.
A hummingbird might drink from my flower.
I might prefer to attract the orange butterfly,
might tip my petals just so, so he sees me,
touches me. I might get sprayed with weed-killer

(I am a wildflower). A heavy boot might
crush me. A kind hand might pluck
me for a bouquet, where I'd smile three days,
then wilt. Drought might kill me, or ice. Or

I might find I like sunshine, might discover
thunderstorms are more fun above-ground,
might pose for a photographer or a painter,
might let down my leaves,
a green waterfall overflowing her dark tower.

HILL COUNTRY SPRING

strip off the ugly brown of drought
and all the green that came so late—
undress—reveal your purple spires—
toss out gold ribbons, bright green fires

—garnet flowers—oh glorious mess
oblivious to sky—say please! say yes!
—drop everything—a musical riot—
a color vibrato—lady, don't hide it!

cloistered love—underneath's inverse
—you've lost control, not one thing forced—
your inhibition—shyness unhorsed

you beckon from down on your knees,
Listen to me—Hear the bees—
late spring bloomer—such a tease

The Descent of the Holy Spirit

LOVE PLANT

Songs 7

He says
You have the voice of an angel

She says
Oh Mr. Cardinal
I have sunflower seeds
Take off your mask

Take my slope, my aspect
Trace every fire trail
Touch the lichen on my tundra
Toggle my wildflower anatomy

And pardon me, as I rush ahead
to the next chapter, for Love
is so like happy death

He says
Take, eat: passionfruit

The Assumption

BEHOLD

I am a mother
who forgot to sing till empty
nested. Mated lo notes
with hi simultaneously.
Ringed days with song.

And you, Sir Flame, you
stand out, fan out that tail,
shift from bead to bead. *Ecce*

Here am I
Here is your chalice of mystery
How can I not drink it all

GOLDEN-CHEEKED WARBLER

She can't quiet down
not while spring is at its peak.
Where oak and cedar meet
she makes her home.

She sports white siderails
with black eyeliner.
Endangered, she's a headliner
found along Edwards Plateau trails.

She's never left Texas.
Her head, golden as the sun.
Her song, should you hear it, stuns.
Her loves, they are reckless.

In tandem she sings gems. Her goal:
Sing cold.
Sing tired.
Sing hungry and whole.

EPHPHATHA

Mark 7:31–37

O my Jesus, take me
aside if you would touch
all my closedness

be gentle
gentle in me all
gone quiet

spit on my hands
which talked for me
through pencil and paper

and please oh please don't
don't let me close me
shut again

HOMECOMING

Songs 8

Almost Easter. Marigolds bloom in full sun.
Like a swallow I return to my mother's house
—her dining room table (the table, the house,
the family, long gone). Seated around the wood,
the Holy Family. Lilies grace the center. *Welcome,*
child, who, with perseverance, walks in the dark.

They were up all night, making music.
It flooded my streets, roared down
my mountains like fire, settled in my garden.
Now I sit: face to face to Holy Face. Sip soup.
Scan cabinets for every bowl, jar, plastic tub
to seal it all up safe.

There is more wine,
Mary says. Jesus says,
Here is bread.
St. Joseph leans close, *Tell us your mysteries. Start with joyful.*

The Coronation of Mary

Bibliography

Anonymous German traditional, *Maria durch ein Dornwald ging,* 1850, *Mary Walked Through a Wood of Thorn,* arranged Philip Radcliffe, Oxford, England: Oxford University Press, 1968.

[Boo Radley] and First Purchase from *To Kill a Mockingbird,* by Harper Lee, Philadelphia: J.B. Lippincott & Co., 1960.

Darlene Love, "Christmas (Baby Please Come Home)," A-side single on *A Christmas Gift for You*, Philles Records, 1963, album.

E.B. White, "Death of a Pig," *The Atlantic*, December 1948, https://www.theatlantic.com/magazine/archive/1948/01/death-pig/309203/.

"I leave my prayers in odd places, too," Jody L. Collins, "What Had Been Lost," *Mining the Bright Birds,* Eugene: Wipf and Stock, 2023. Used by permission of Wipf and Stock.

"It Was a Beauteous Evening, Calm and Free," William Wordsworth, *Poems, in Two Volumes*, (London: Longman, Hurst, and Orme, Paternoster-Row, 1807.

John Grady Cole, Jimmy Blevins, unnamed wife of Jimmy Blevins, Jimmy Blevins Gospel Hour from *All the Pretty Horses*, Cormac McCarthy, New York City: Alfred A. Knopf, 1992.

"Letter XV to Céline: 2 August 1893, "*The Story of a Soul: The Autobiography of St. Thérèse of Lisieux*, Thérèse of Lisieux, ed. Mother Agnes of Jesus, Gastonia: TAN, 2010.

"Make Me River," "Make Me Chalice," "Make Me Sheet Moss," "Make Me Willow," "Make Me Cello," "Make Me Red-tailed Hawk," "Make Me Plow Blade," Abigail Carroll, *Habitation of Wonder*, Eugene: Wipf and Stock, 2018. Used by permission of Wipf and Stock.

"Man steals heart, no charges filed," law enforcement report, *Fredericksburg Standard-Radio Post*, March 6, 2024.

A Scriptural Rosary for the Family, compiled by Father Bernard Mulchahy, New Haven, O.P. Knights of Columbus Supreme Council, 2007-2023.

"Stopping by Woods on a Snowy Evening," Robert Frost, *The Poetry of Robert Frost*, ed. by Edward Connery Lathem, New York City: Henry Holt and Company, 1969.

"Wintering," Sylvia Plath, *Ariel*, ed. by Ted Hughes, London: Faber and Faber, 1965.

FLAGLESS MEMORIAL DAY

Psalm 30
for my spiritual director

When I was sinking down, sinking down, sinking down
(and didn't know it, though I sang the hymn),
Lord, you veered me to the hiding place,
reoriented my shoulder away from so shiny a pile of shards.
I asked my new friend to tea, Lord, and she came!
Lord, you helped me cross that flagless memorial day
with black tea blended with local lavender.
We ate farm-fresh blackberries and my homemade oat bread.
O Lord, you heard me
confess to her my thorns, my dreams, my revelations.
She saw the hallway in my wall—
what you, Lord, knew needed to open wide.
We've met every month since. Lord,
that was a decade ago.

And Lord, you know I still strive nights on the couch,
still spill my backpack of music down the pew,
startled one so love-sick gets to sing joy
in the morning, in the house of the Lord.

POMEGRANATE

Her penance: peel a pomegranate,
bring tough skin to heel.
    She eats the arils one by one,
    a pencil in her hand.
    She eats until they all are none,
    until she writes a land
    that's filled with pomegranate trees
    who sway in pomegranate breeze.
No synonym will suffice. She
savors each sweet-tart wave.

www.ingramcontent.com/pod-product-compliance
Lightning Source LLC
Chambersburg PA
CBHW060420050426
42449CB00009B/2048